Piano - Vocal - Guitar

The Best of Diana Krall

Front cover photo by Bruce Weber

ISBN 0-634-06332-4

HAL•LEONARD®
CORPORATION

7777 W. BLUEMOUND RD. P.O. BOX 13819 MILWAUKEE, WI 53213

Visit Hal Leonard Online at
www.halleonard.com

CONTENTS

ALL OR NOTHING AT ALL

Words by JACK LAWRENCE
Music by ARTHUR ALTMAN

lost be-yond re-call._____ The kiss in your eyes, the

touch of your hand makes me weak,_____ and my

heart may grow diz-zy and fall. And if I

fell un-der the spell of your call,_____

BÉSAME MUCHO
(Kiss Me Much)

Music and Spanish Words by
CONSUELO VELAZQUEZ
English Words by SUNNY SKYLAR

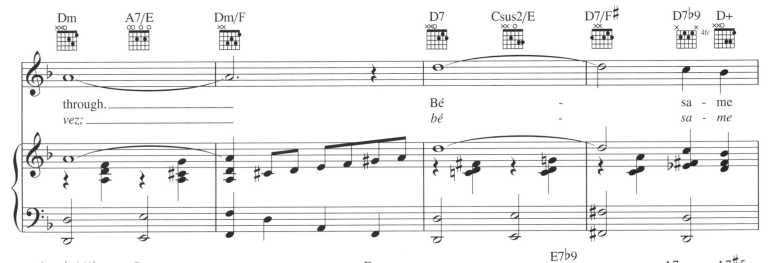

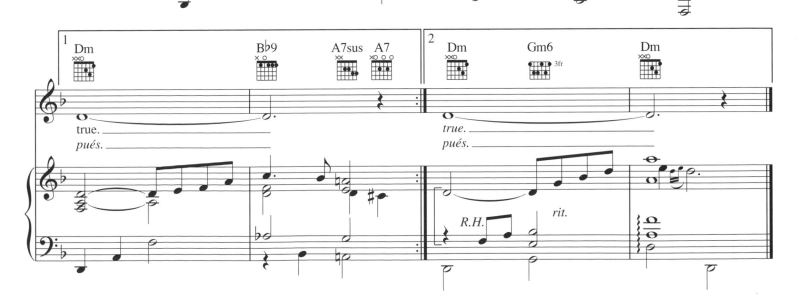

BETWEEN THE DEVIL AND THE DEEP BLUE SEA

Lyric by TED KOEHLER
Music by HAROLD ARLEN

A BLOSSOM FELL

Words and Music by HOWARD BARNES,
HAROLD CORNELIUS and DOMINIC JOHN

A blos-som fell _____ from off a

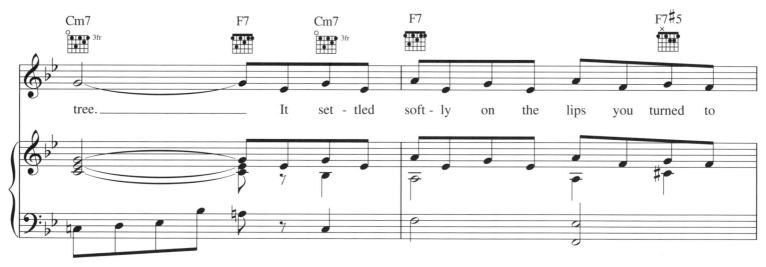

tree. _____ It set-tled soft-ly on the lips you turned to

me. _____ The gyp-sies say, and I know

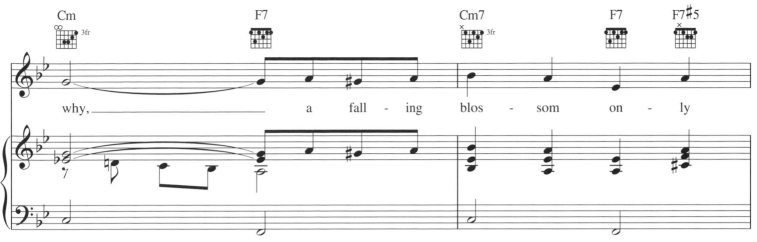

why, _____ a fall - ing blos - som on - ly

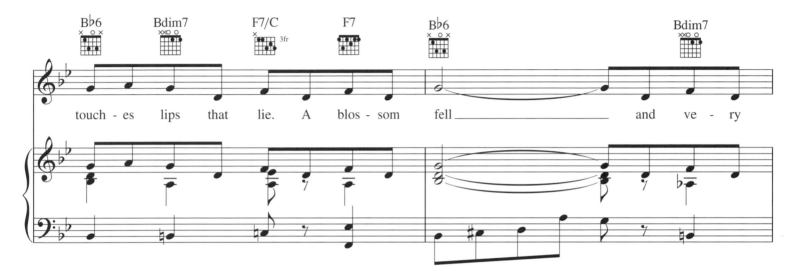

touch - es lips that lie. A blos - som fell _____ and ve - ry

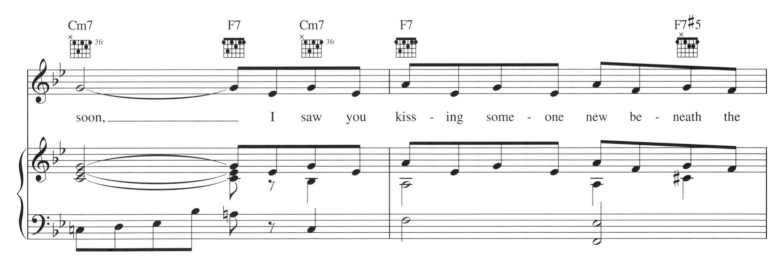

soon, _____ I saw you kiss - ing some - one new be - neath the

moon. _____ I thought you loved me. _____ You said you

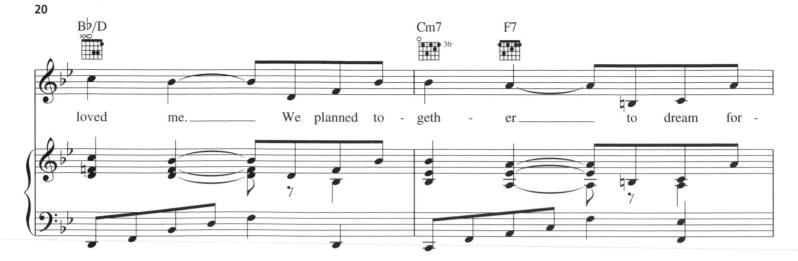

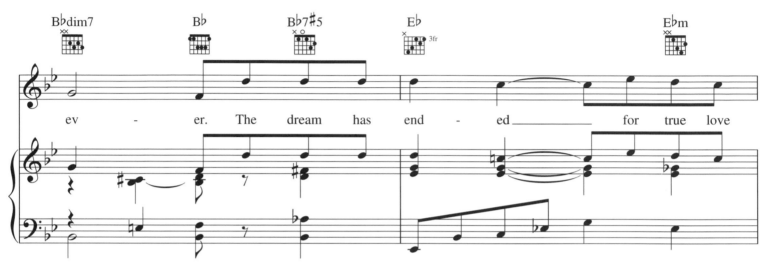

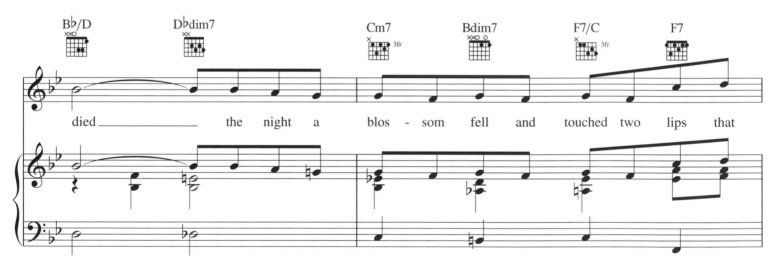

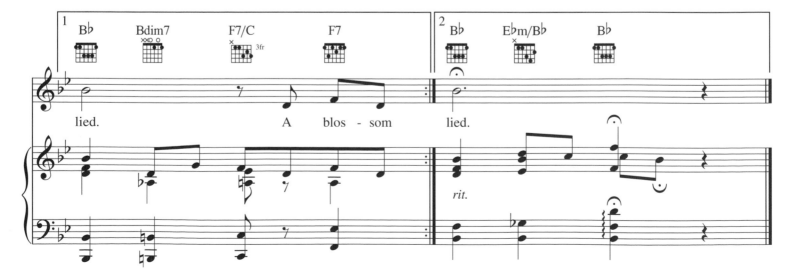

BODY AND SOUL

Words by EDWARD HEYMAN,
ROBERT SOUR and FRANK EYTON
Music by JOHN GREEN

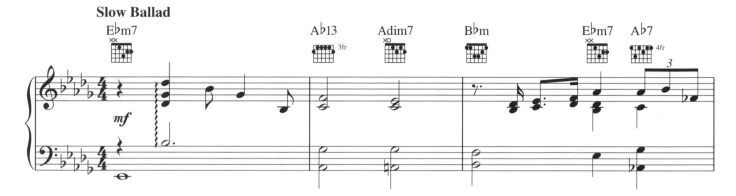

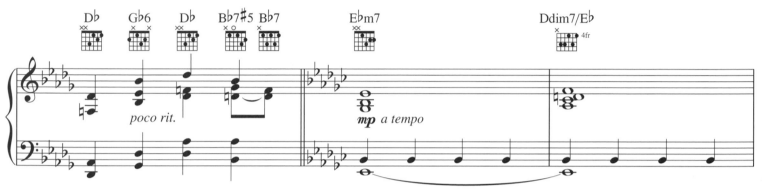

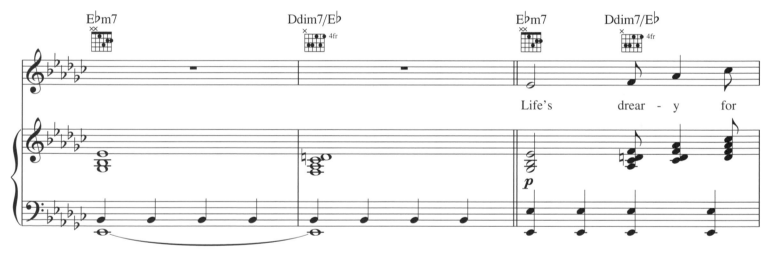

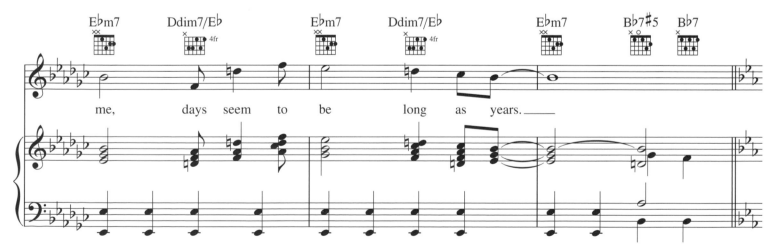

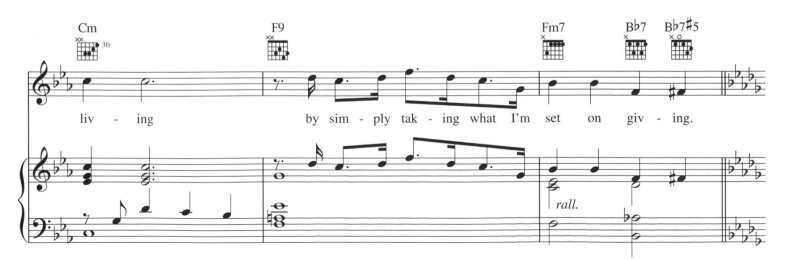

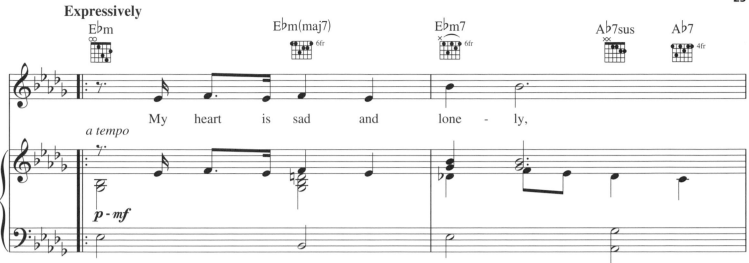

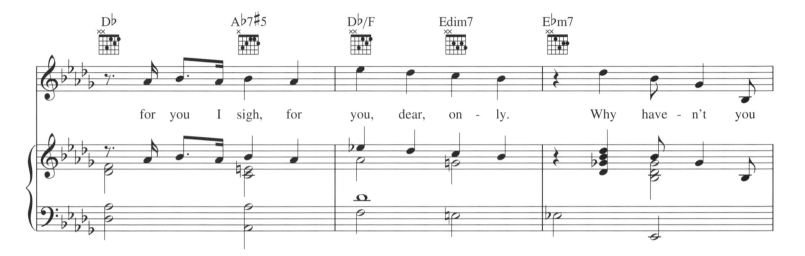

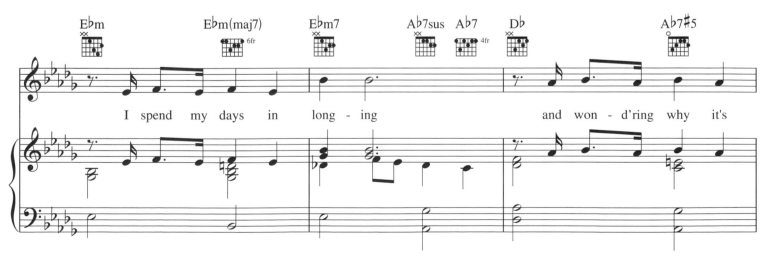

me you're wrong - ing, I tell you I mean it,

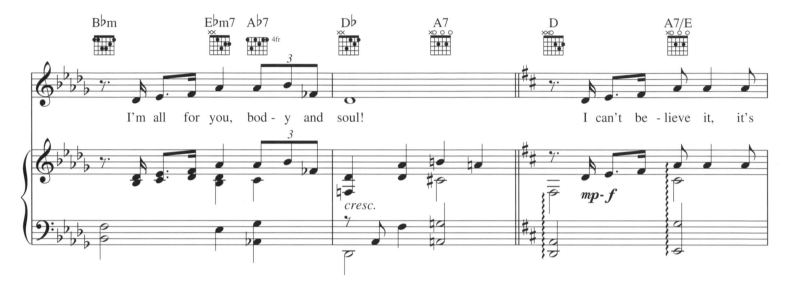

I'm all for you, bod - y and soul! I can't be - lieve it, it's

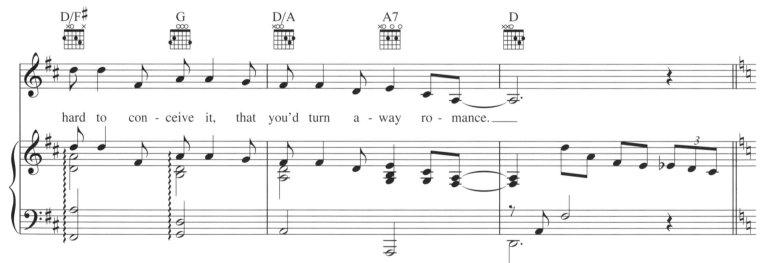

hard to con - ceive it, that you'd turn a - way ro - mance._____

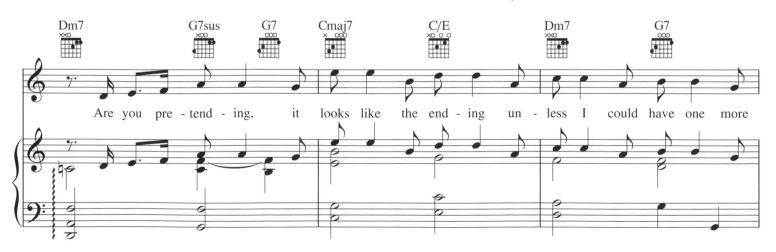

Are you pre - tend - ing, it looks like the end - ing un - less I could have one more

25

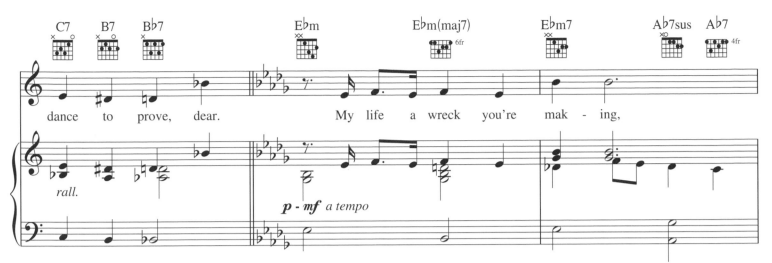

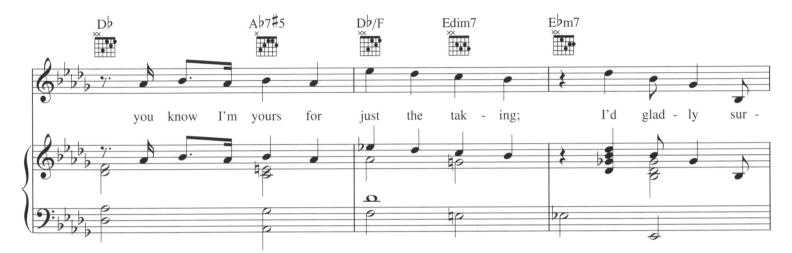

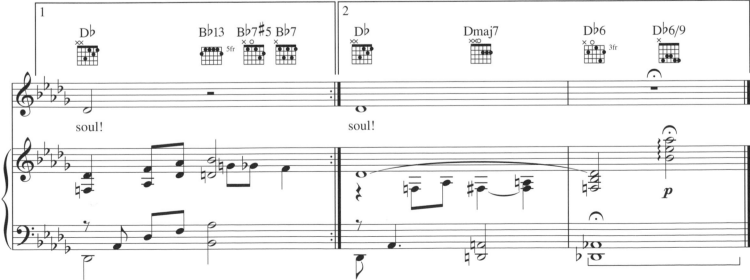

BROADWAY

Words and Music by BILL BYRD,
TEDDY McRAE and HENRI WOODE

Moderato

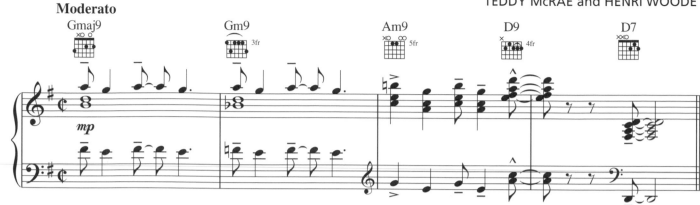

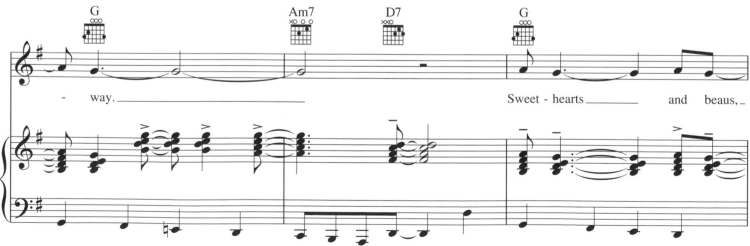

Broad-way, _____ Broad-way, _____ ev-'ry-bo-dy's hap-py _____ and gay _____ where the night is bright-er _____ than day _____ all a-long Broad- way. _____ Sweet-hearts _____ and beaus, _

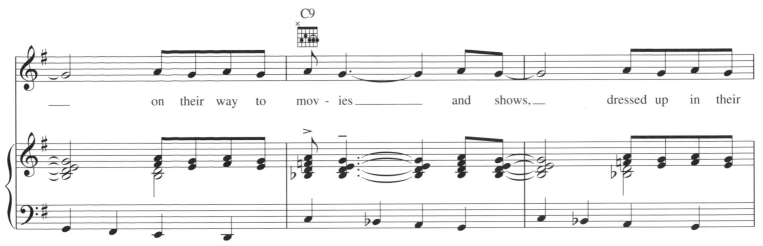

on their way to mov - ies _____ and shows, _ dressed up in their

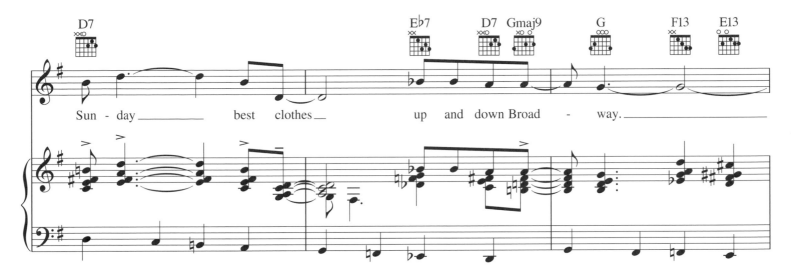

Sun - day _____ best clothes _ up and down Broad - way. _____

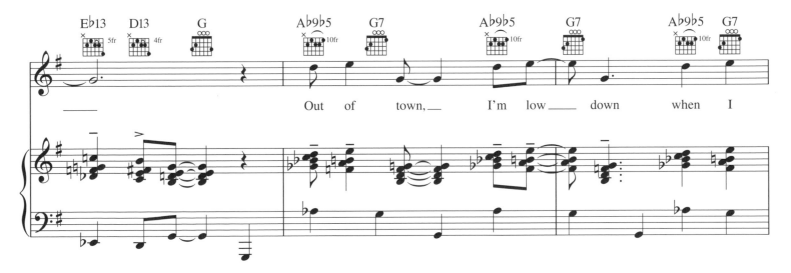

_ Out of town, _ I'm low _ down when I

walk a - long the main street. _____ An - y - where _ I don't _

28

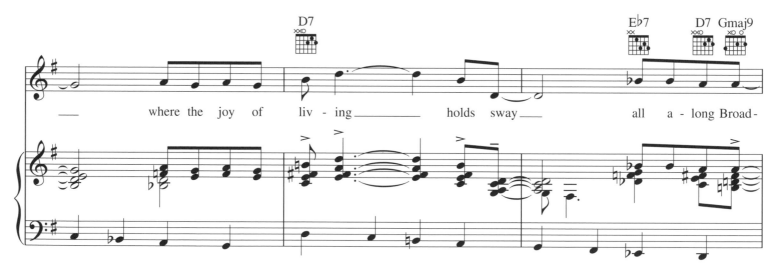

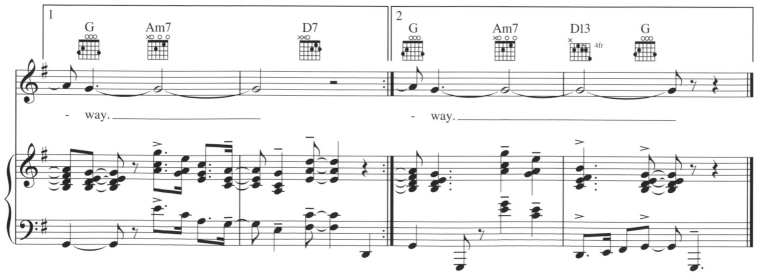

CRY ME A RIVER

Words and Music by
ARTHUR HAMILTON

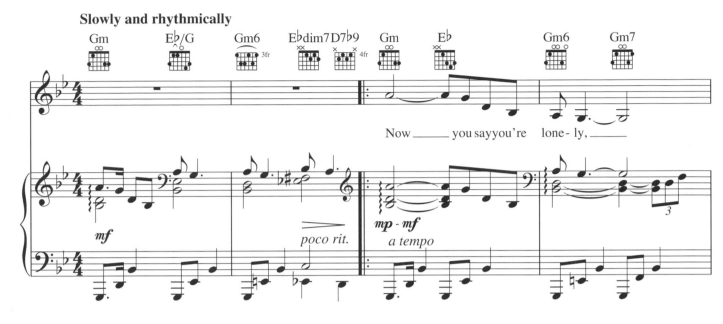

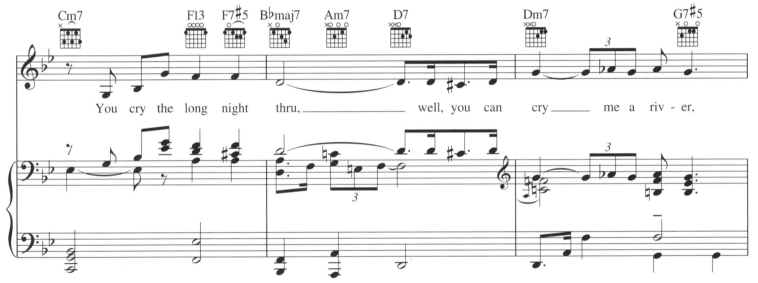

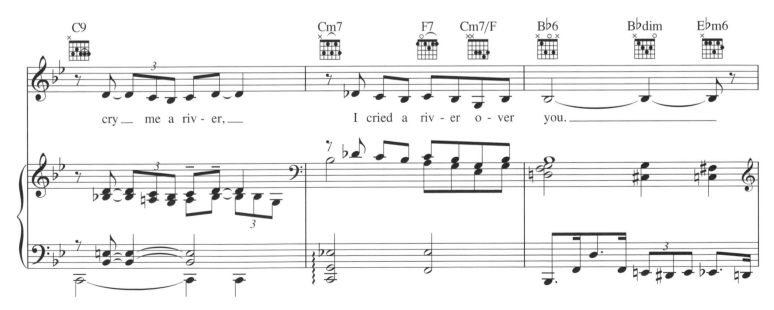

Ped.

DO NOTHIN' TILL YOU HEAR FROM ME

Words and Music by DUKE ELLINGTON
and BOB RUSSELL

Moderately Slow

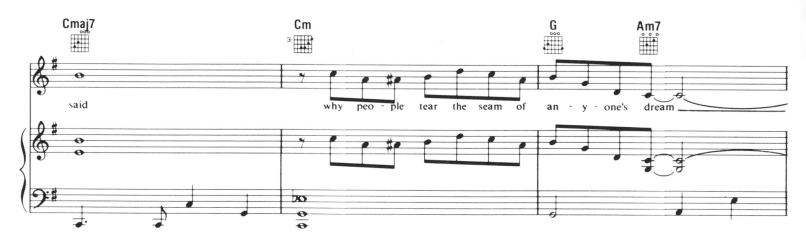

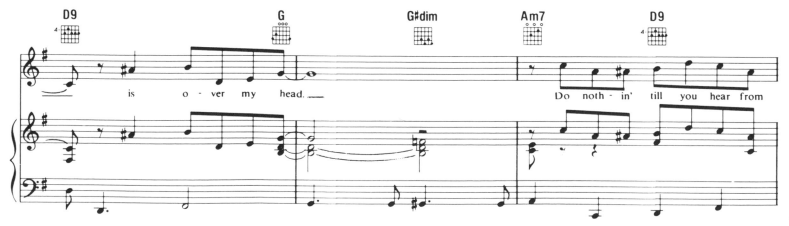

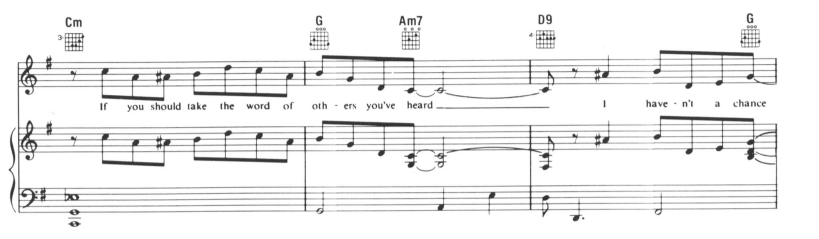

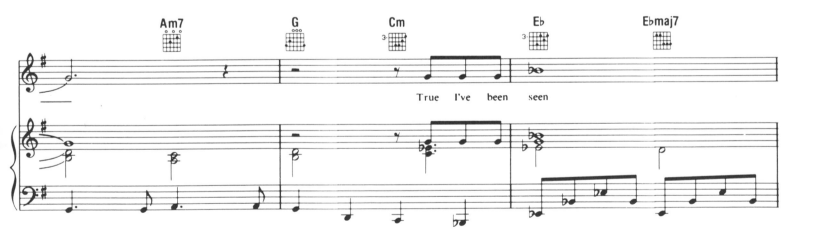

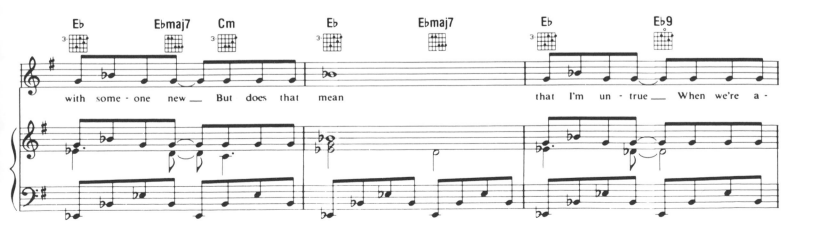

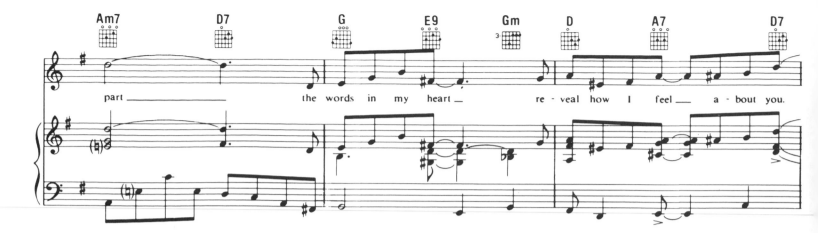

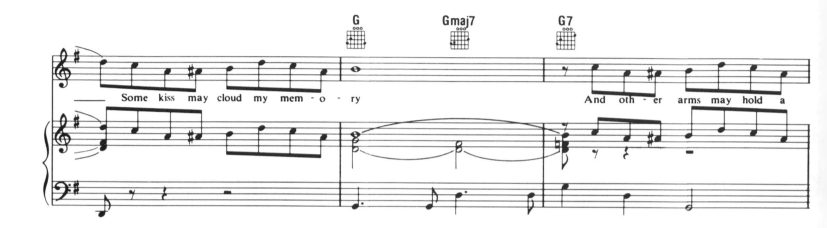

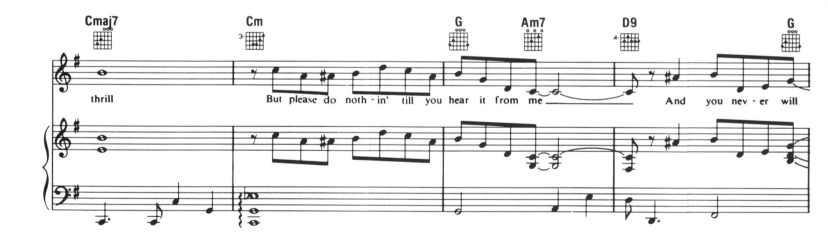

HOW DEEP IS THE OCEAN
(How High Is the Sky)

Words and Music by
IRVING BERLIN

THE FRIM FRAM SAUCE

Words and Music by JOE RICARDEL
and REDD EVANS

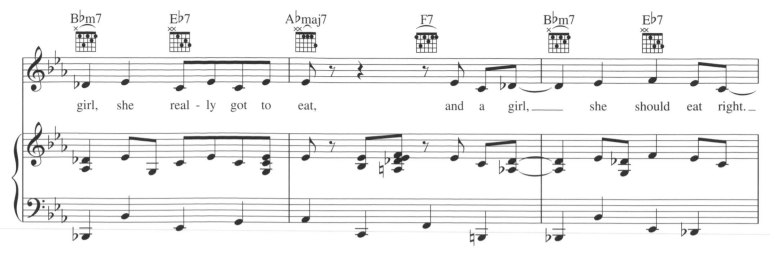

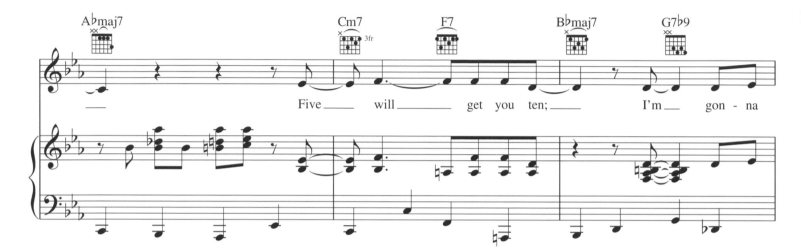

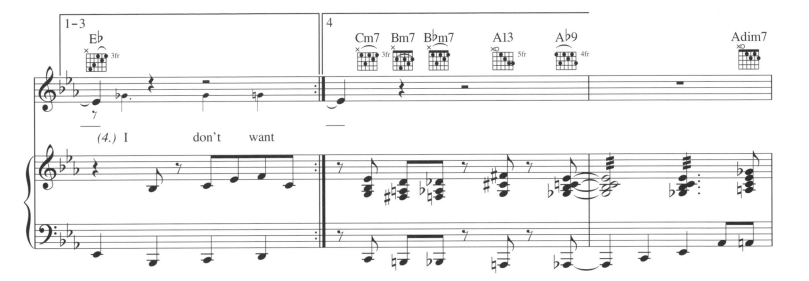

GEE BABY, AIN'T I GOOD TO YOU

Words by DON REDMAN
and ANDY RAZAF
Music by DON REDMAN

Slow blues

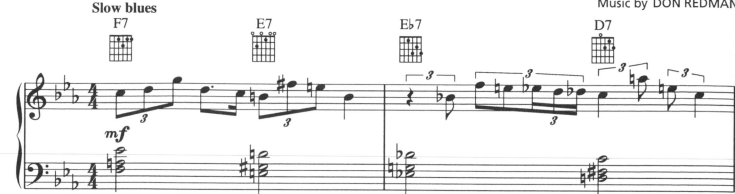

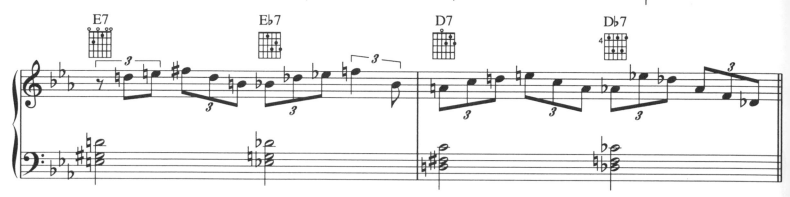

Love _____ makes me treat you the way _____ that I do.

Gee ba-by, ain't I good _ to you! There's noth - in' too good for a

I DON'T STAND A GHOST OF A CHANCE

Words by BING CROSBY and NED WASHINGTON
Music by VICTOR YOUNG

Moderately, Singable

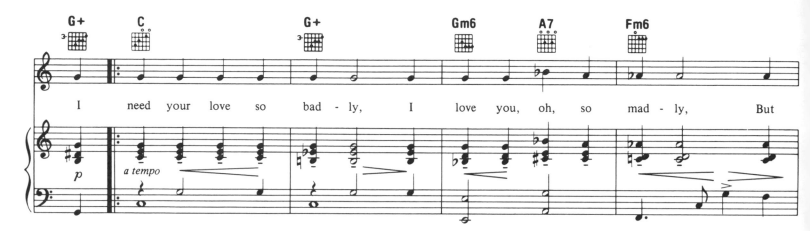

I need your love so bad-ly, I love you, oh, so mad-ly, But

I don't stand A Ghost Of A Chance with you!_____ I

thought at last I'd found you, But oth-er loves sur-round you, And

I GET ALONG WITHOUT YOU VERY WELL
(Except Sometimes)

Words and Music by HOAGY CARMICHAEL
Inspired by a poem written by J.B. THOMPSON

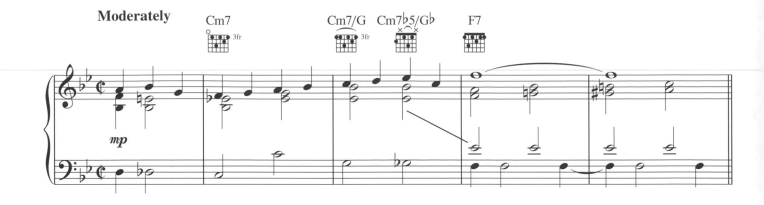

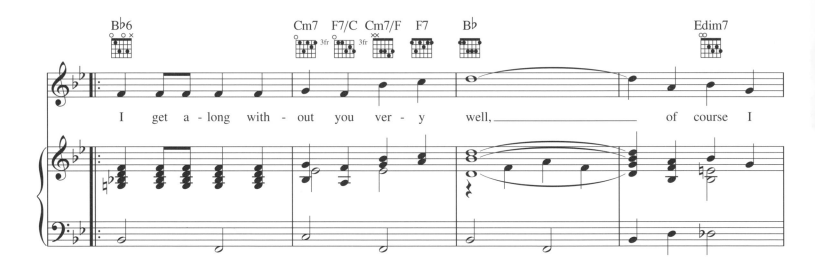

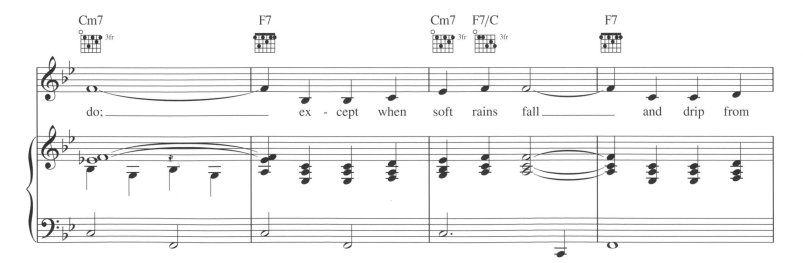

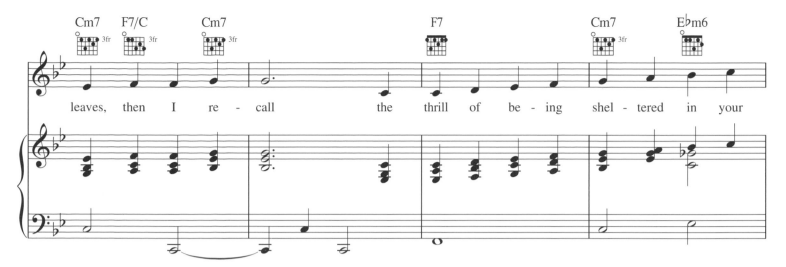

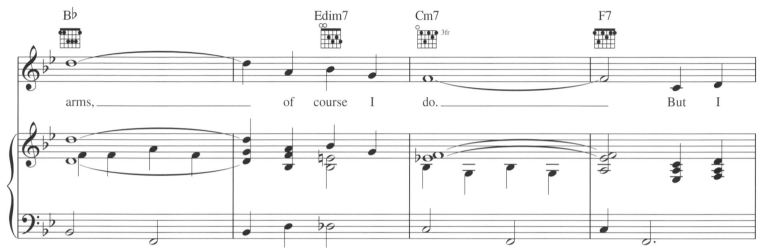

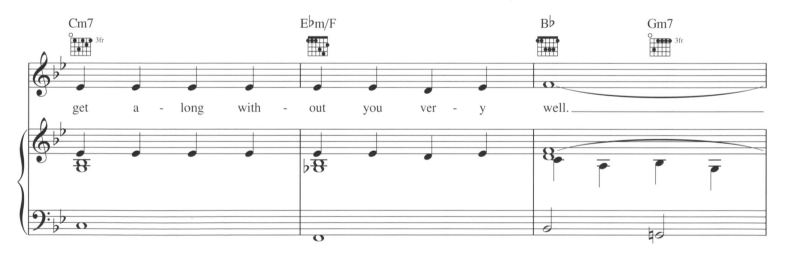

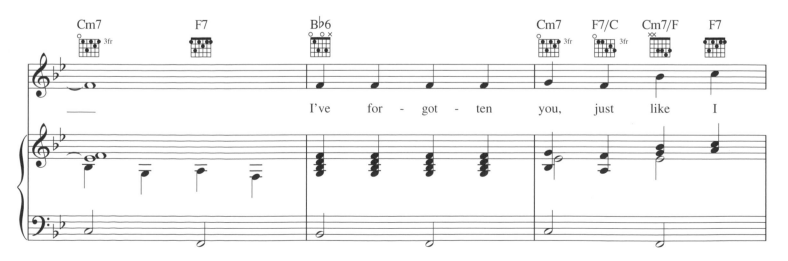

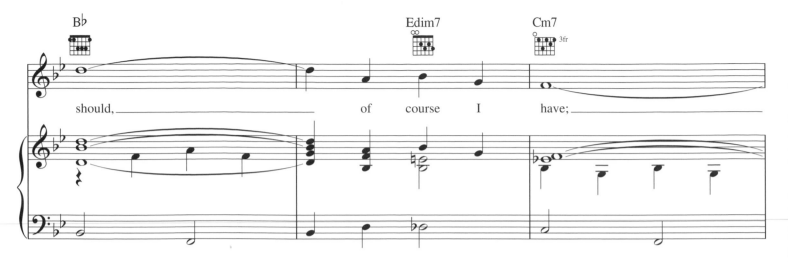

should,_____ of course I have;_____

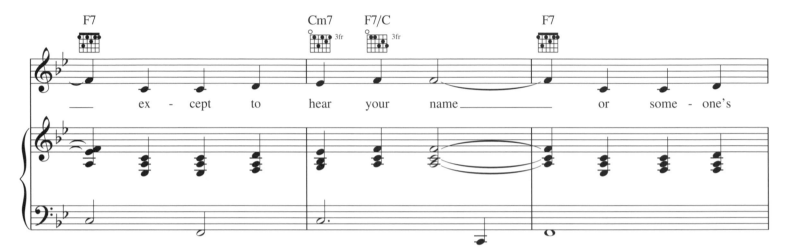

____ ex - cept to hear your name_____ or some - one's

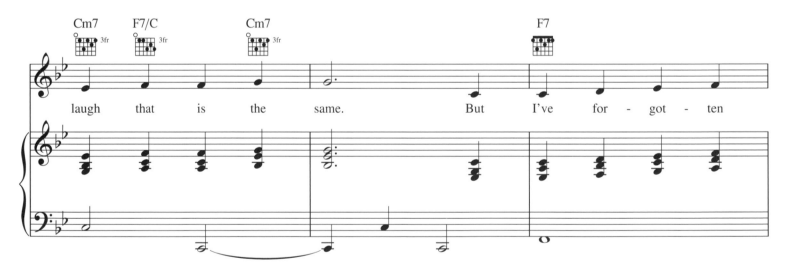

laugh that is the same. But I've for - got - ten

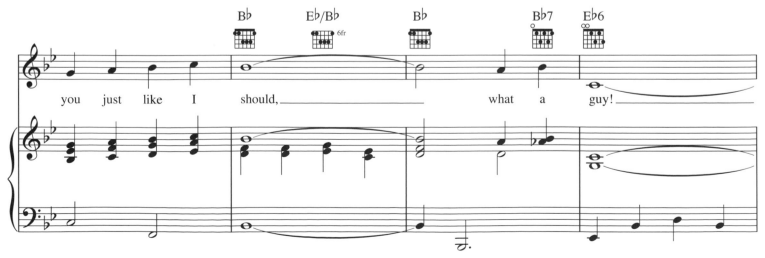

you just like I should,_____ what a guy!_____

What a fool am I _____ to think my break-ing heart ____

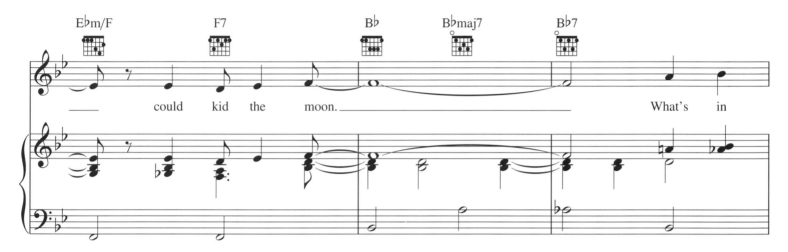

____ could kid the moon. _____ What's in

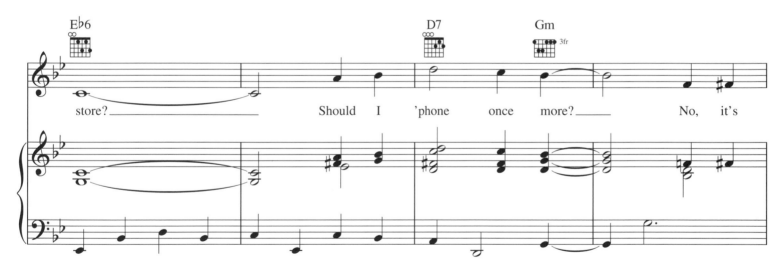

store? _____ Should I 'phone once more? ____ No, it's

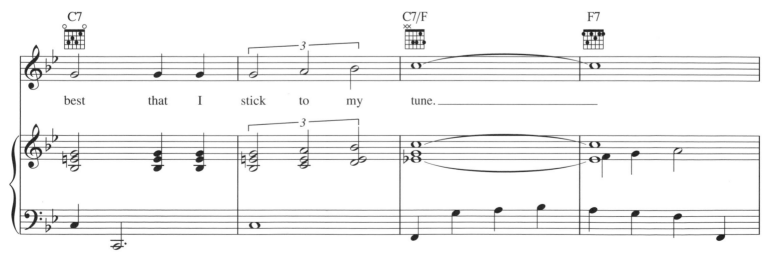

best that I stick to my tune. _____

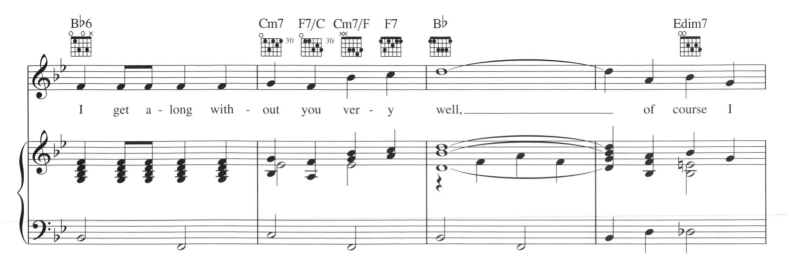

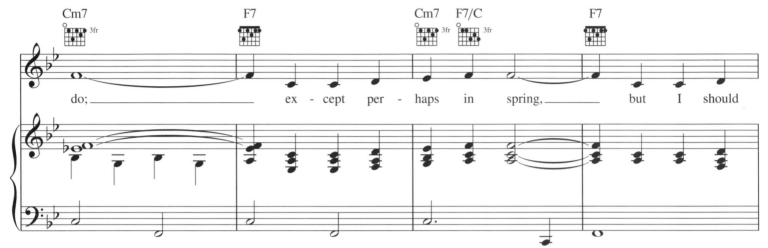

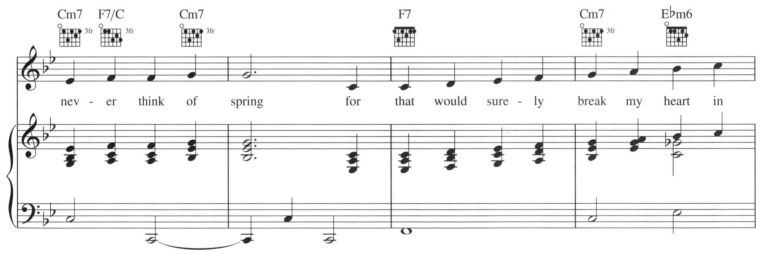

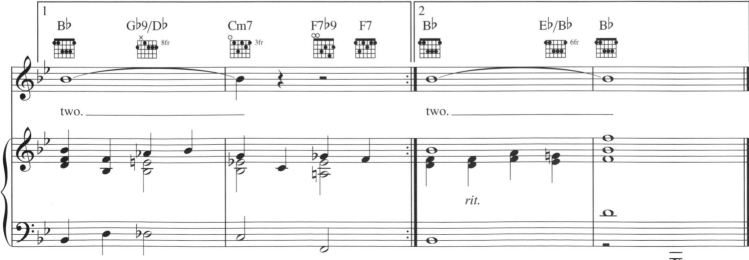

I'M JUST A LUCKY SO AND SO

Words by MACK DAVID
Music by DUKE ELLINGTON

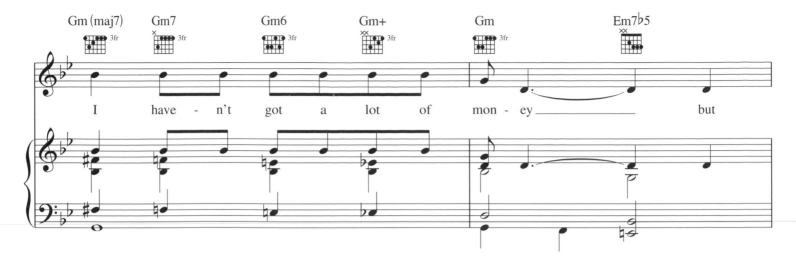

I have-n't got a lot of mon-ey _____ but

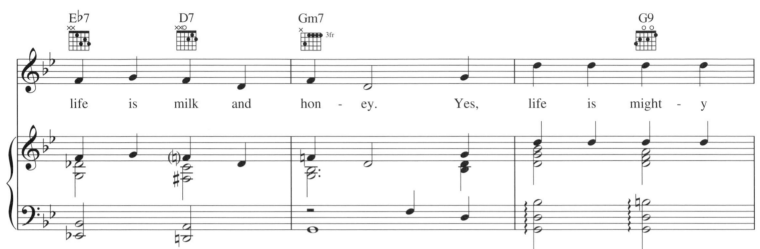

life is milk and hon-ey. Yes, life is might-y

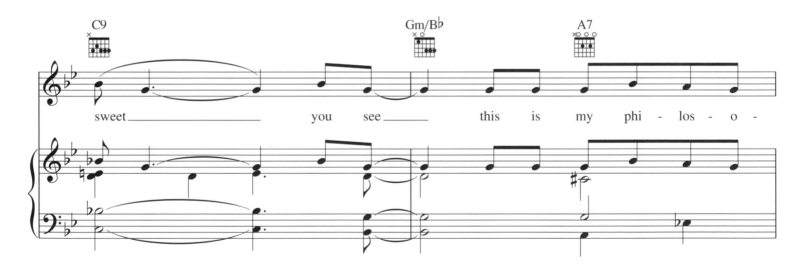

sweet _____ you see _____ this is my phi-los-o-

phy. As I walk down the street ___ seems ev-'ry-one I meet ___

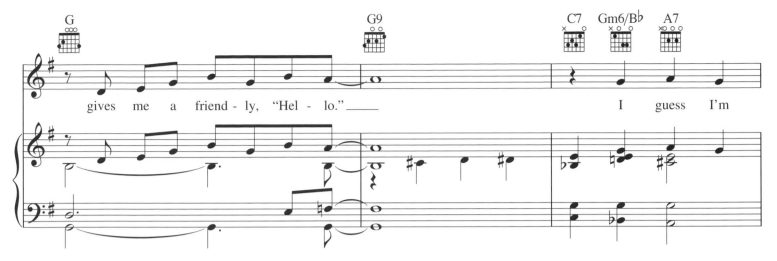

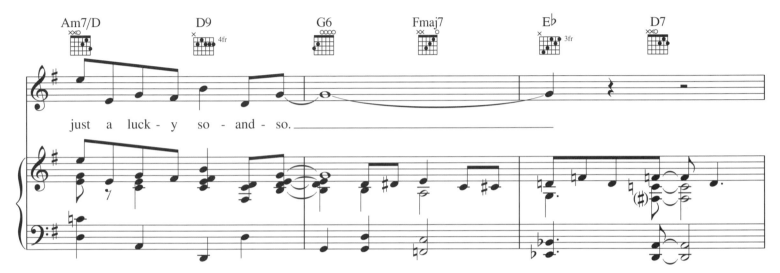

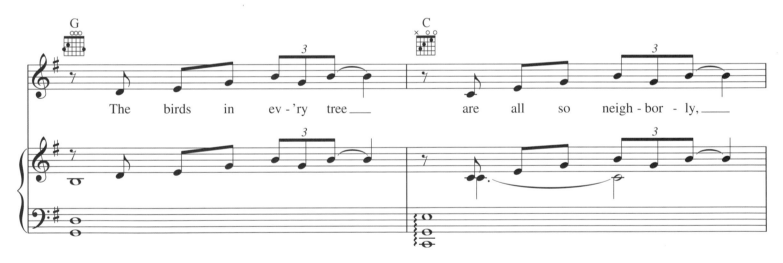

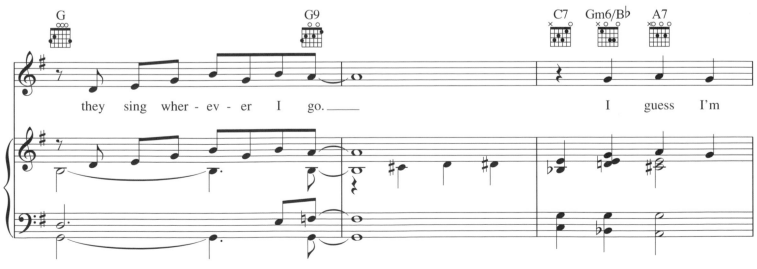

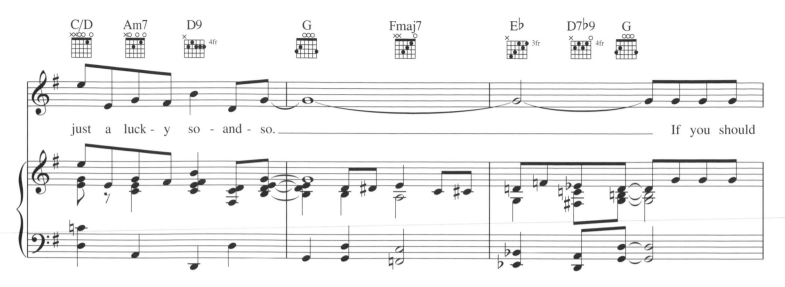

just a luck - y so - and - so._____ If you should

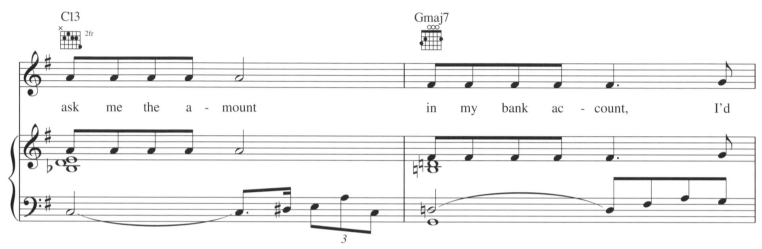

ask me the a - mount in my bank ac - count, I'd

have to con - fess____ that I'm slip - pin',_____ but

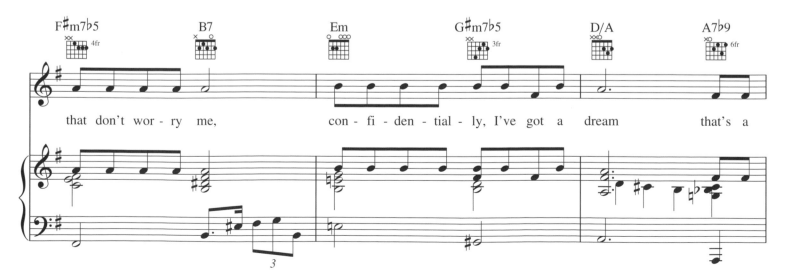

that don't wor - ry me, con - fi - den - tial - ly, I've got a dream that's a

pip-pin'._____ And when the day is through___ each night I hur-ry to___

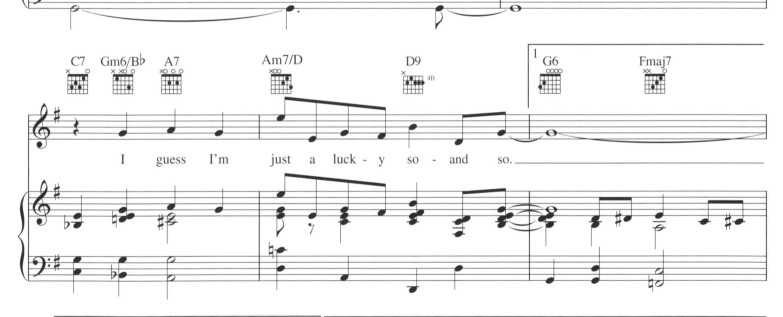

a home where love waits, I know._____

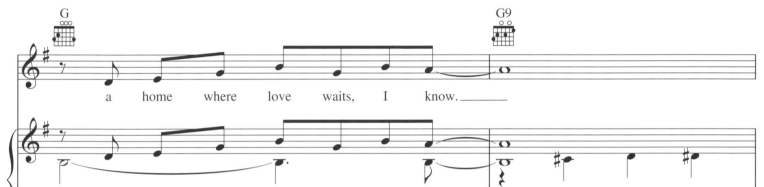

I guess I'm just a luck-y so-and so._____

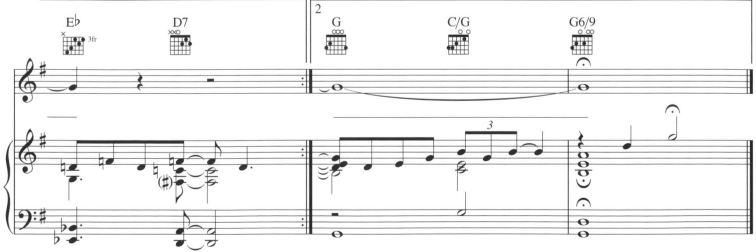

I REMEMBER YOU

from the Paramount Picture THE FLEET'S IN

Words by JOHNNY MERCER
Music by VICTOR SCHERTZINGER

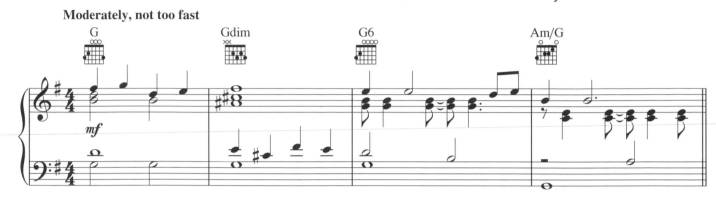

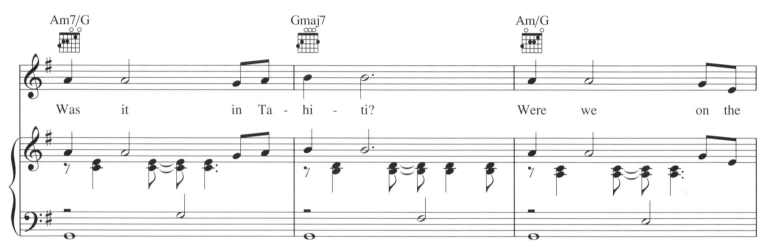

Was it in Ta - hi - ti? Were we on the

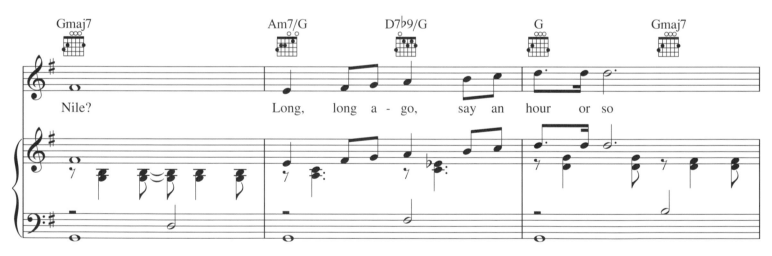

Nile? Long, long a - go, say an hour or so

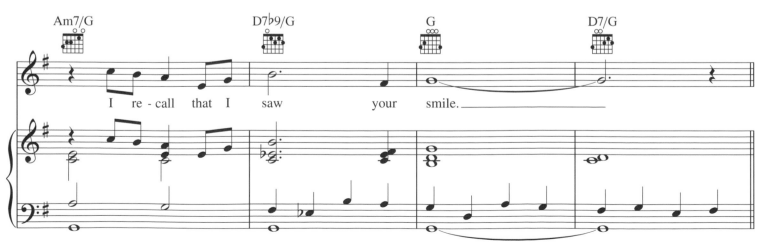

I re - call that I saw your smile. _____

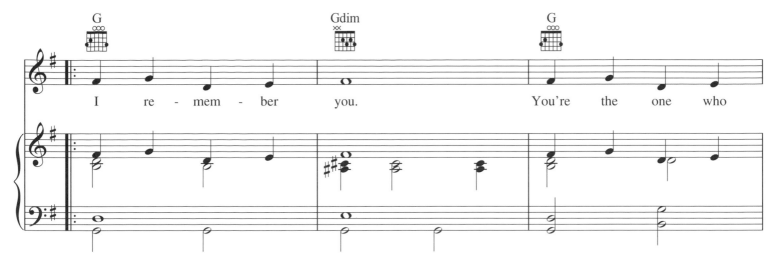

I re - mem - ber you. You're the one who

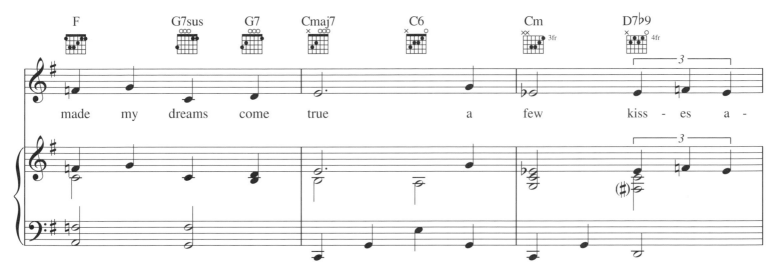

made my dreams come true a few kiss - es a -

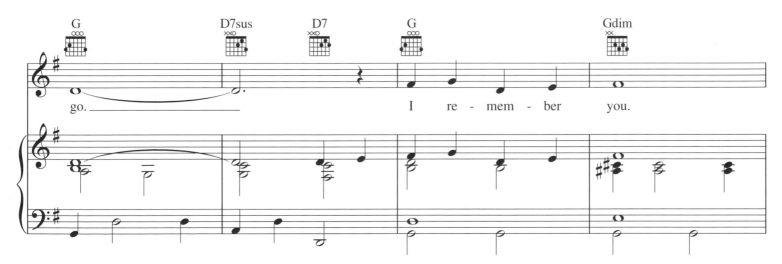

go. I re - mem - ber you.

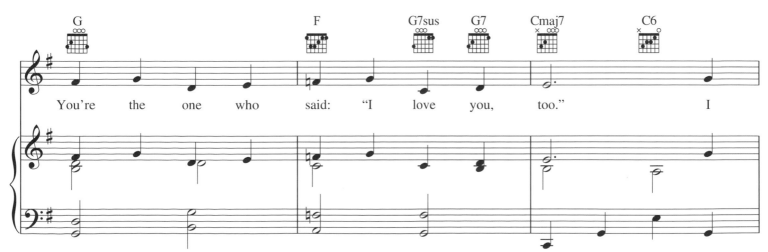

You're the one who said: "I love you, too." I

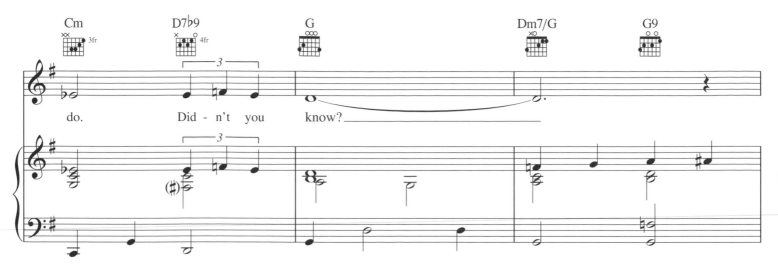

do. Did - n't you know? _____

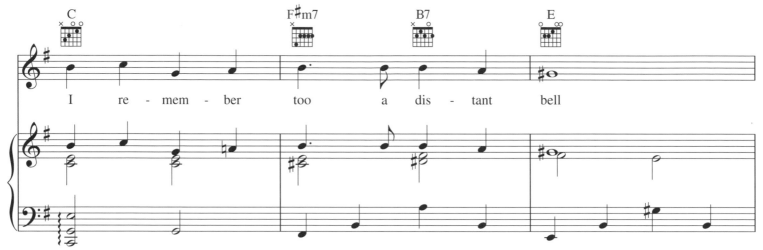

I re - mem - ber too a dis - tant bell

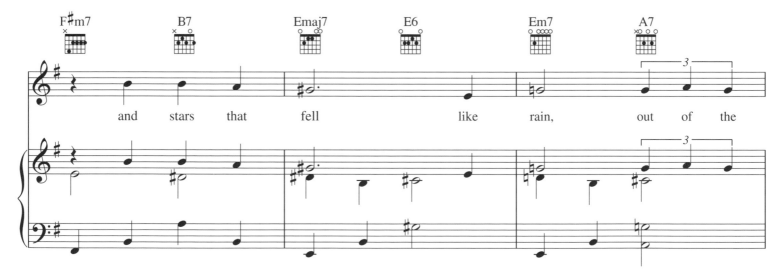

and stars that fell like rain, out of the

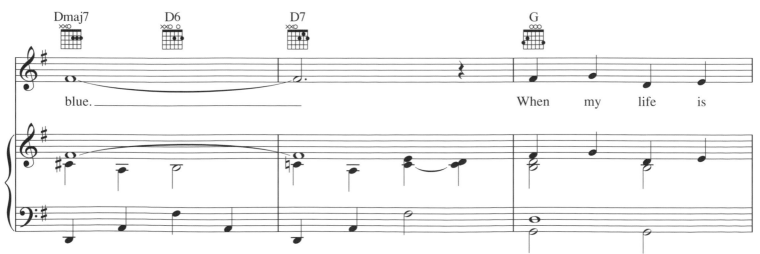

blue. _____ When my life is

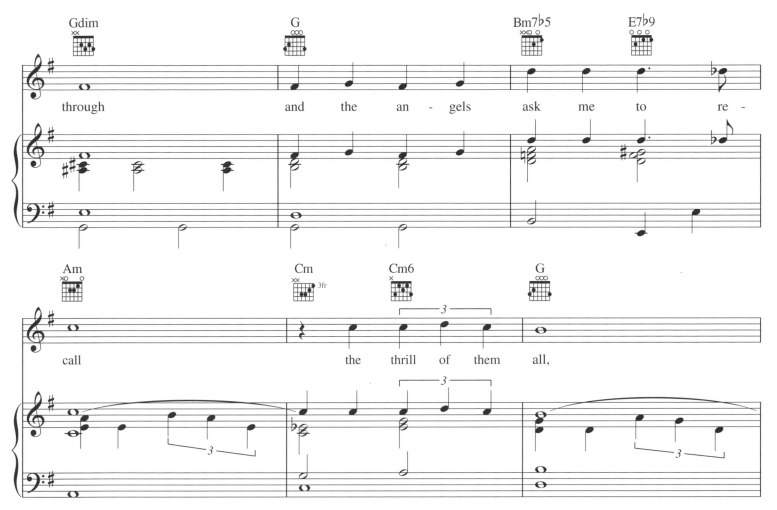

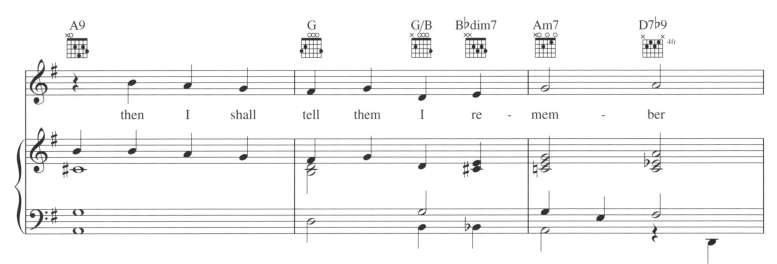

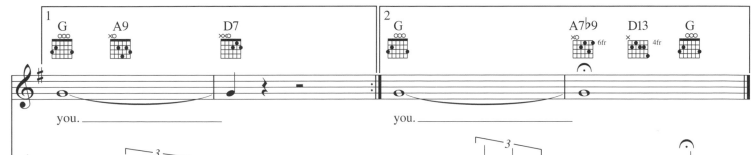

I'VE GOT THE WORLD ON A STRING

Lyric by TED KOEHLER
Music by HAROLD ARLEN

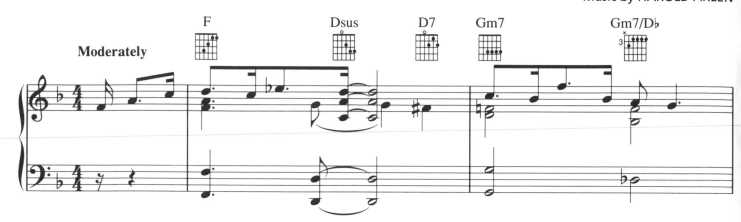

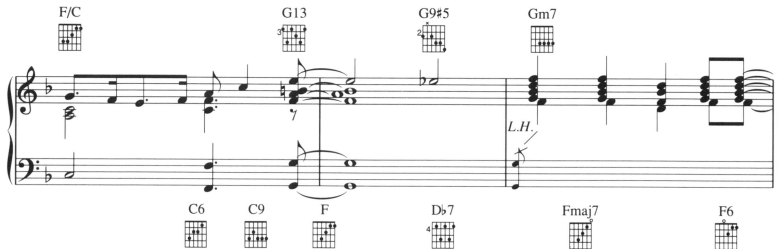

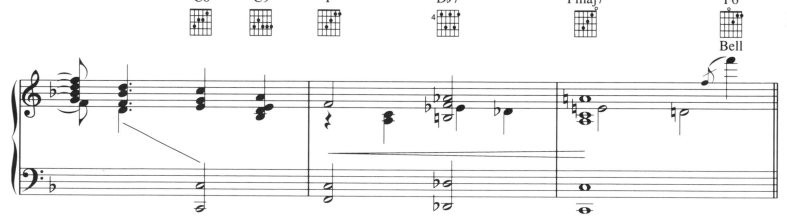

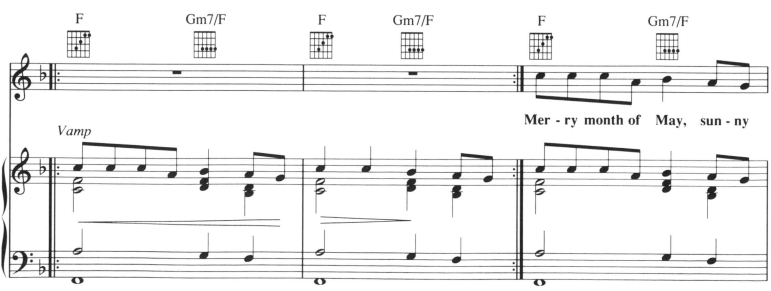

Mer - ry month of May, sun - ny

LET'S GET LOST

from the Paramount Picture HAPPY GO LUCKY

Words by FRANK LOESSER
Music by JIMMY McHUGH

LET'S FACE THE MUSIC AND DANCE

from the Motion Picture FOLLOW THE FLEET

Words and Music by
IRVING BERLIN

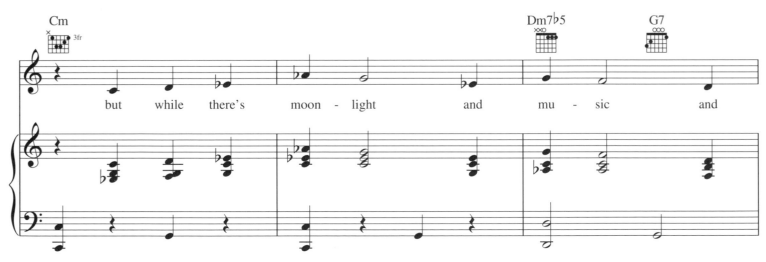

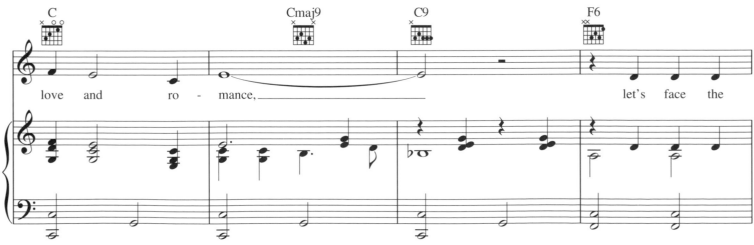

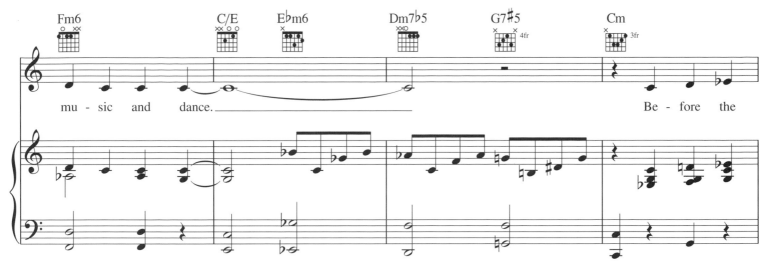

mu - sic and dance._____ Be - fore the

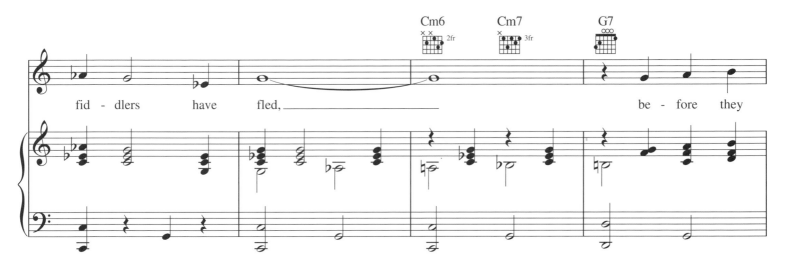

fid - dlers have fled,_____ be - fore they

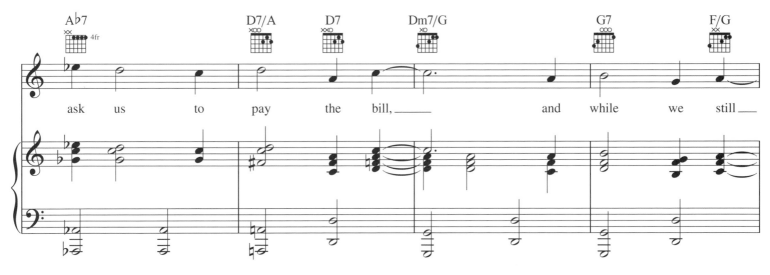

ask us to pay the bill,_____ and while we still___

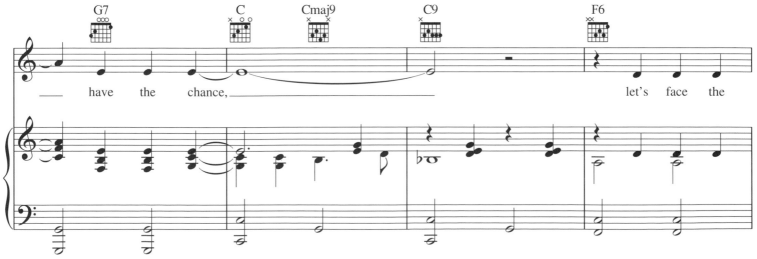

___ have the chance,_____ let's face the

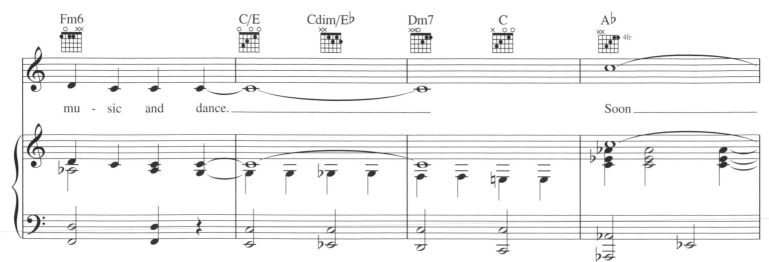

mu - sic and dance._____ Soon _____

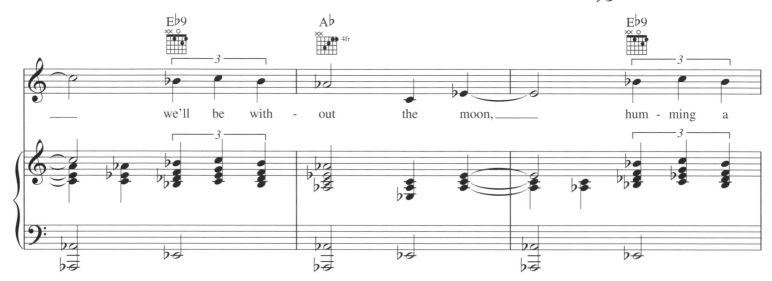

_____ we'll be with - out the moon,_____ hum - ming a

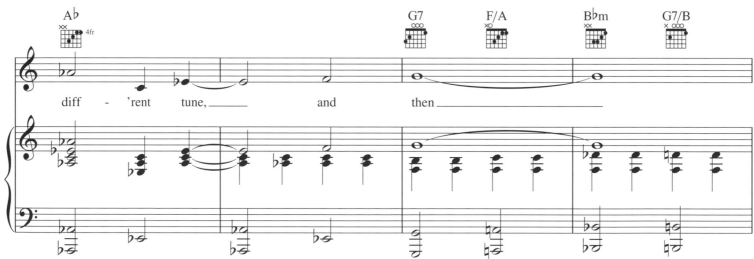

diff - 'rent tune,_____ and then _____

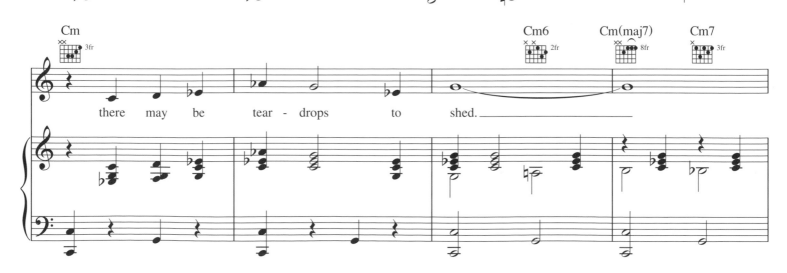

there may be tear - drops to shed._____

LOST MIND

Words and Music by
PERCY MAYFIELD

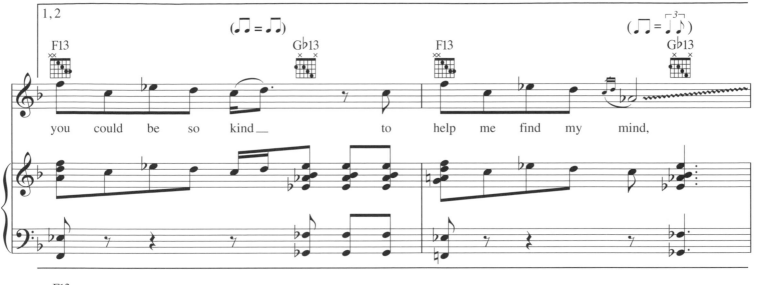

PEEL ME A GRAPE

Words and Music by
DAVE FRISHBERG
Arranged for piano by
DAVE FRISHBERG

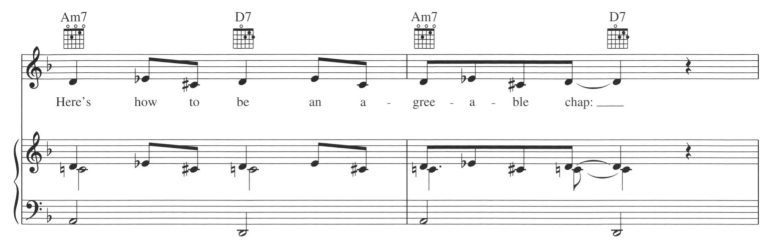

Here's how to be an a - gree - a - ble chap: ___

Love me and leave me in lux - u - ry's lap. ___ Hop when I hol - ler,

D.S. al Coda

skip when I snap. ___ When I say, "Do it," jump to it.

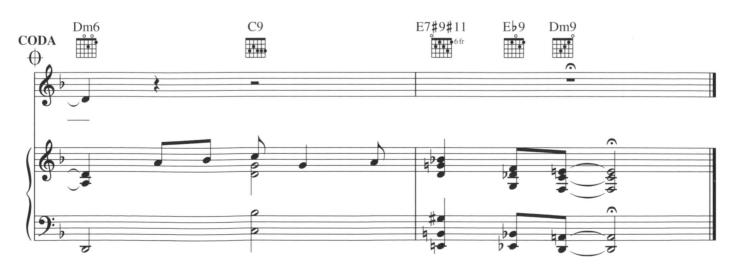

CODA

LOVE LETTERS
Theme from the Paramount Picture LOVE LETTERS

Words by EDWARD HEYMAN
Music by VICTOR YOUNG

Moderately slow, with expression

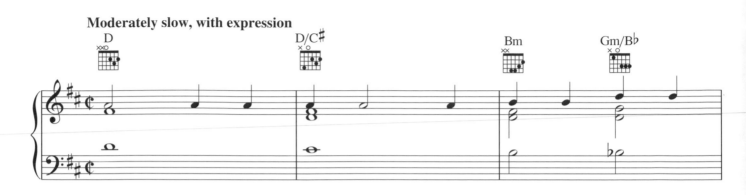

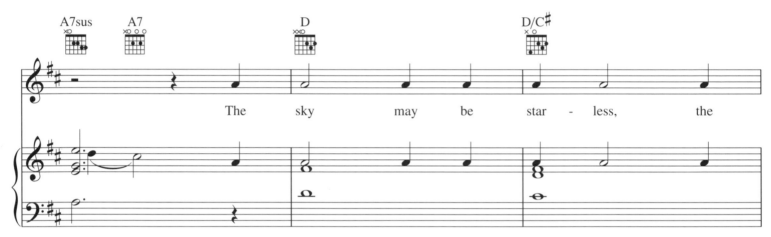

The sky may be star - less, the

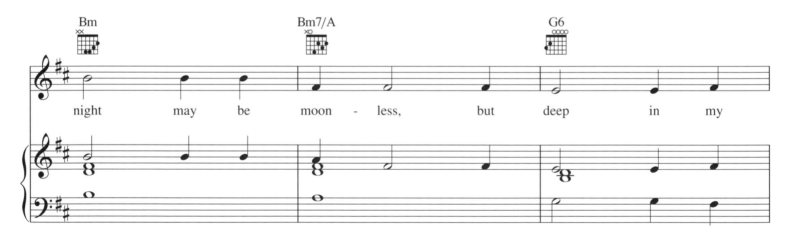

night may be moon - less, but deep in my

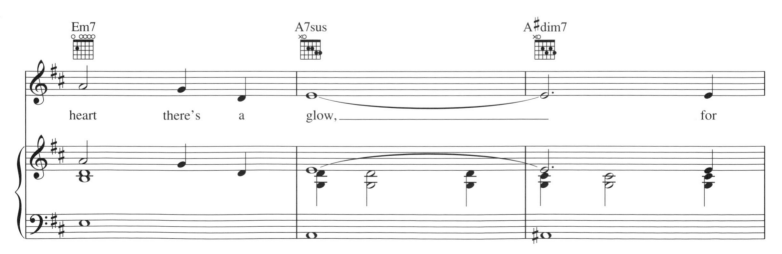

heart there's a glow, _____ for

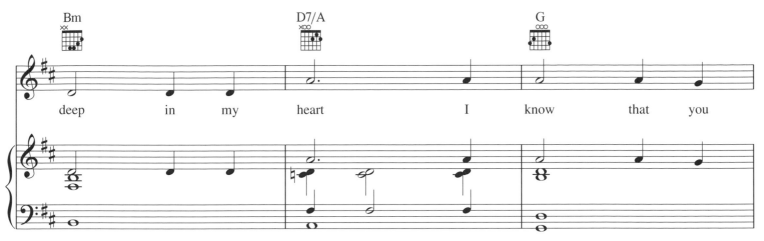

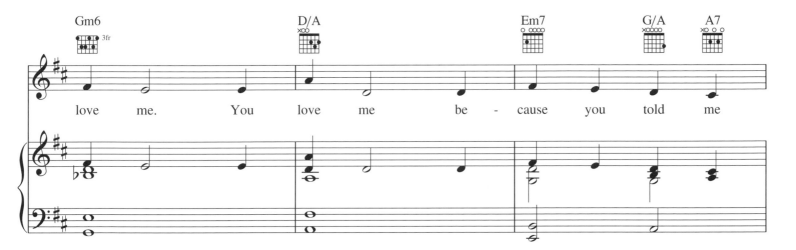

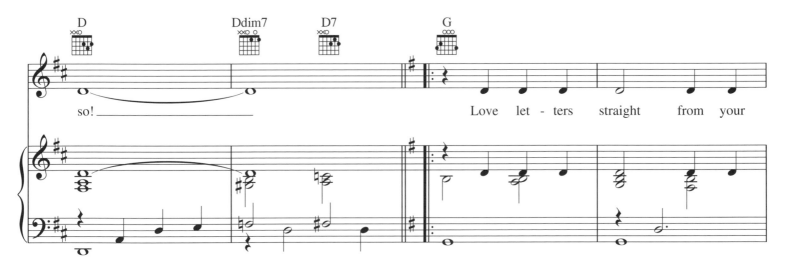

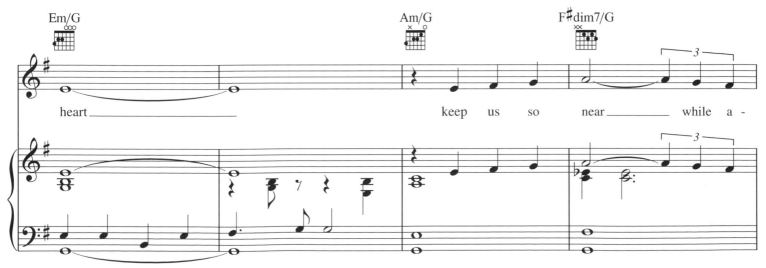

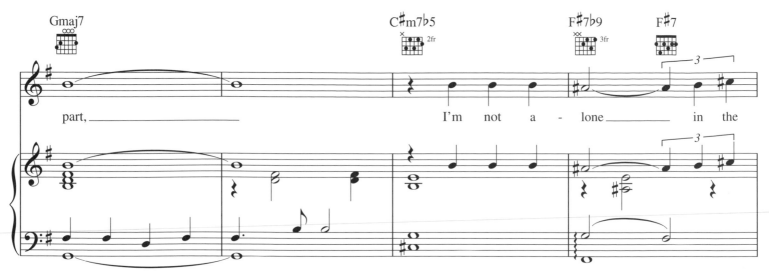

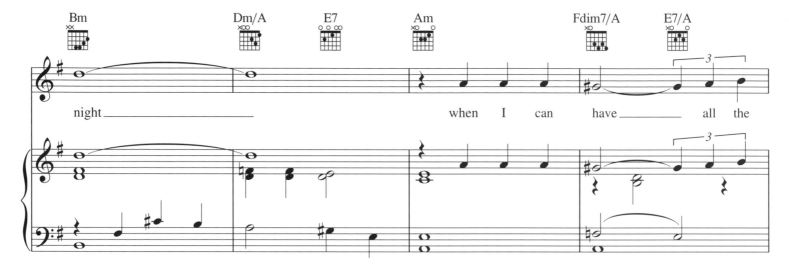

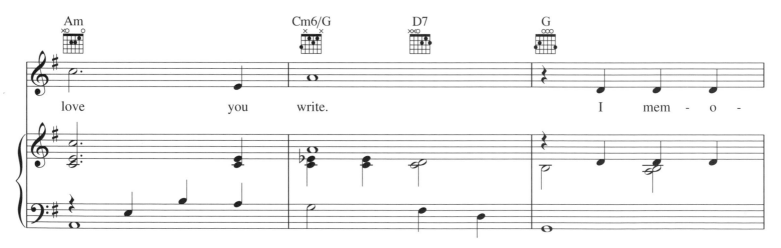

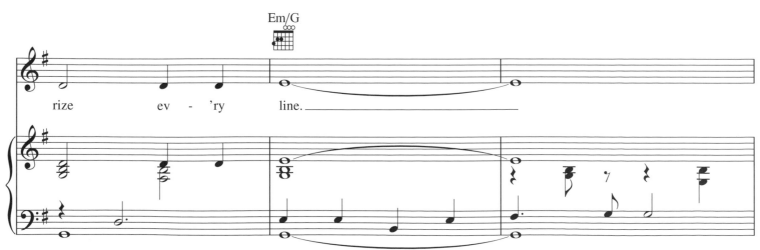

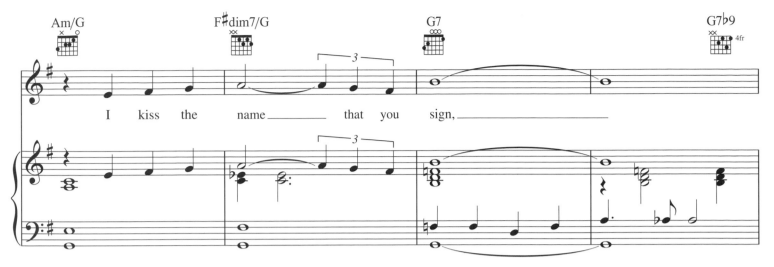

I kiss the name _____ that you sign, _____

And, dar - ling, then I read a - gain right from the

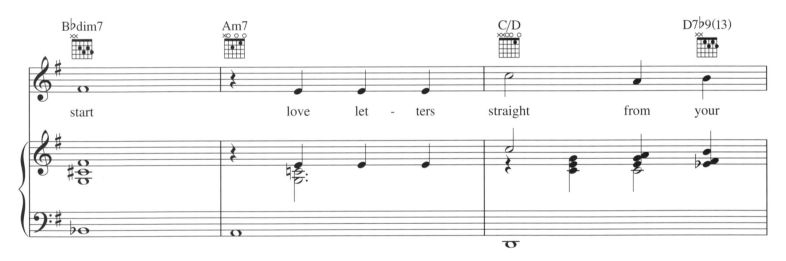

start love let - ters straight from your

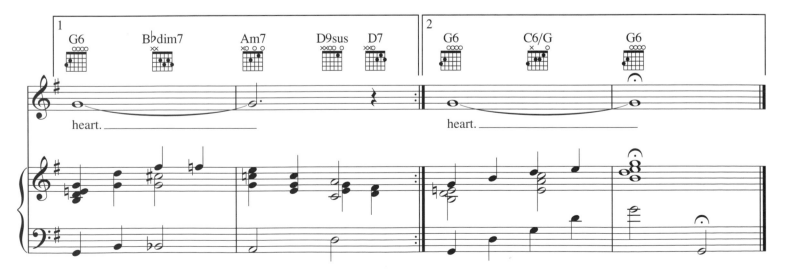

heart. _____   heart. _____

ONLY TRUST YOUR HEART

Words by SAMMY CAHN
Music by BENNY CARTER

STRAIGHTEN UP AND FLY RIGHT

Words and Music by NAT KING COLE
and IRVING MILLS

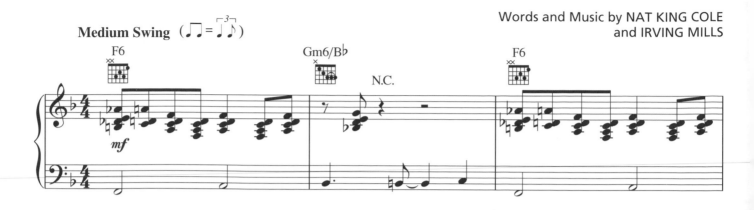

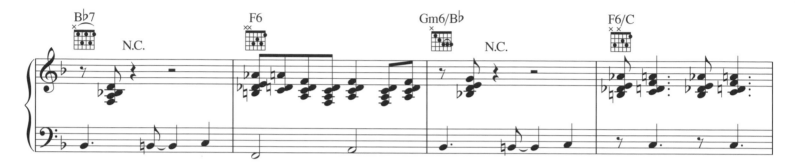

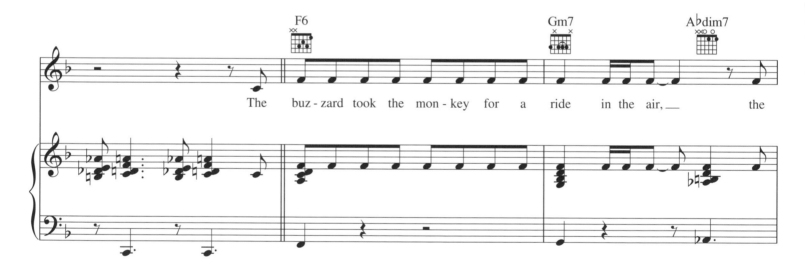

The buz-zard took the mon-key for a ride in the air, ___ the

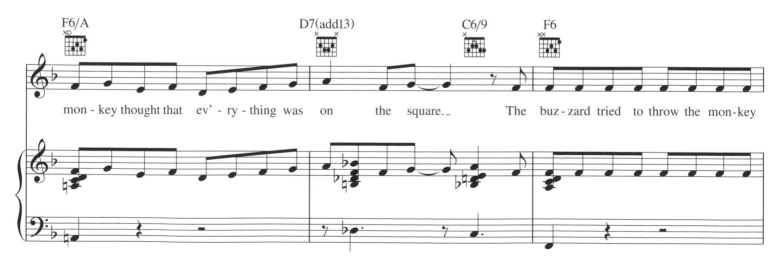

mon-key thought that ev'-ry-thing was on the square.___ The buz-zard tried to throw the mon-key

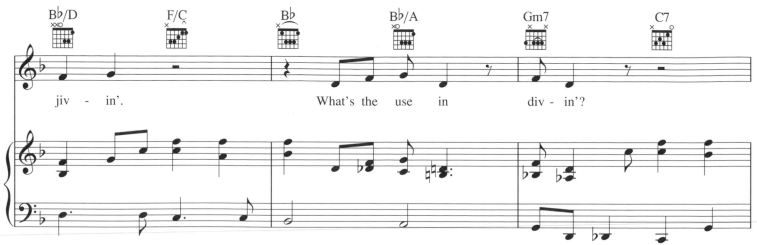

jiv - in'. What's the use in div - in'?

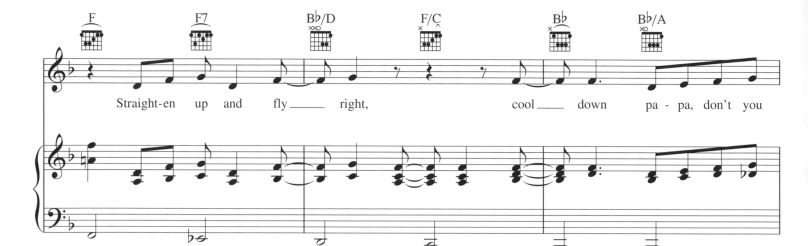

Straight-en up and fly ____ right, cool ____ down pa - pa, don't you

blow your top." ____ The buz - zard told the mon - key, "You're ____ chok - ing me, ____ re -

lease your hold ____ and I'll set you free." ____ The mon - key looked the buz - zard right

dead   in the eye __ and said, "Your   sto - ry's touch ing, but it   sounds __ like a   lie."

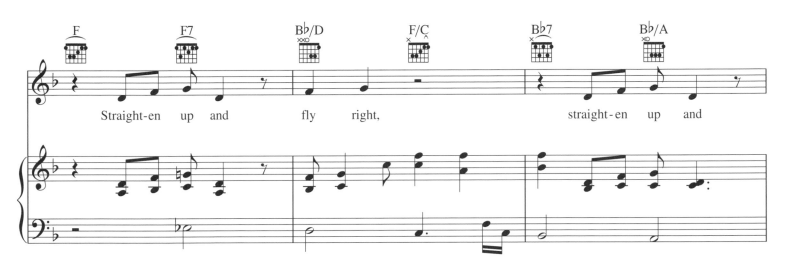

Straight-en up and   fly   right,   straight-en up and

do right.   Straight-en   up and fly ___ right,   cool __

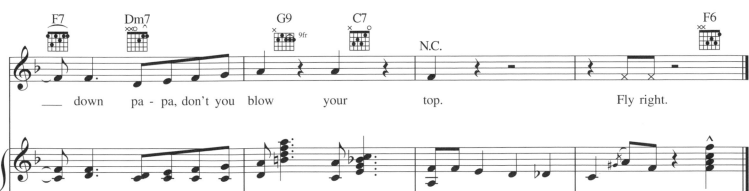

__ down pa - pa, don't you blow   your   top.   Fly right.

YOU CALL IT MADNESS
(But I Call It Love)

Words and Music by CON CONRAD, GLADYS DUBOIS
RUSS COLUMBO and PAUL GREGOR

Suavely

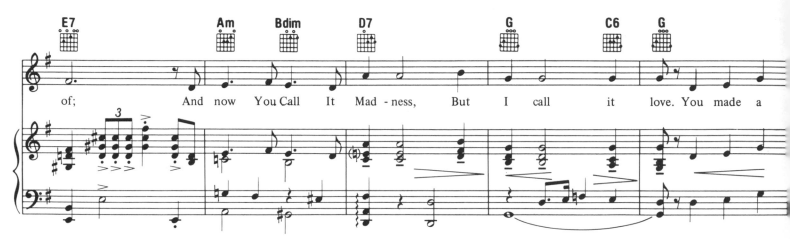

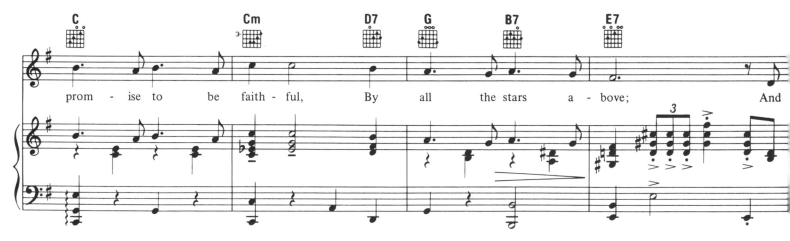

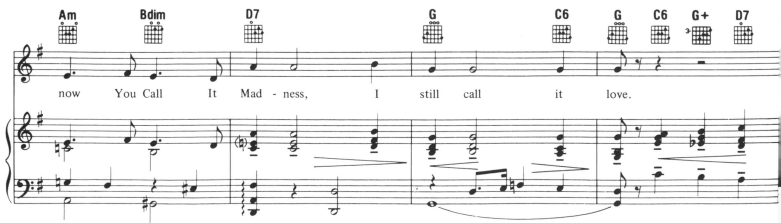

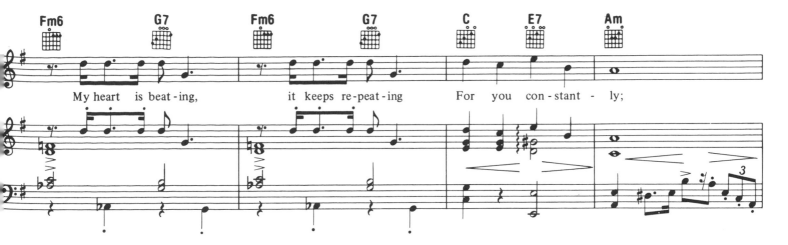

My heart is beat-ing, it keeps re-peat-ing For you con-stant-ly;

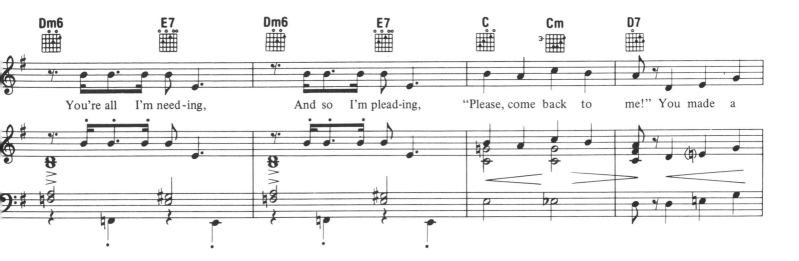

You're all I'm need-ing, And so I'm plead-ing, "Please, come back to me!" You made a

play - thing out of ro - mance! What do you know of love? That's

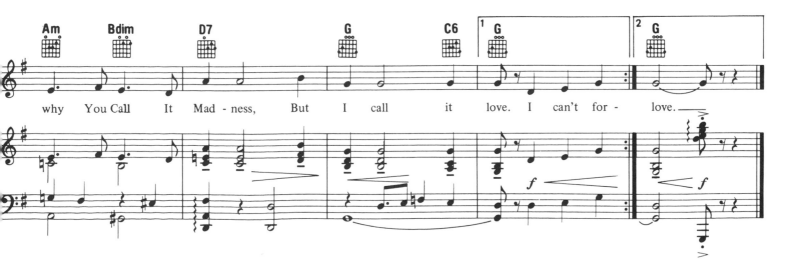

why You Call It Mad - ness, But I call it love. I can't for - love.

THIS CAN'T BE LOVE
from THE BOYS FROM SYRACUSE

Words by LORENZ HART
Music by RICHARD RODGERS

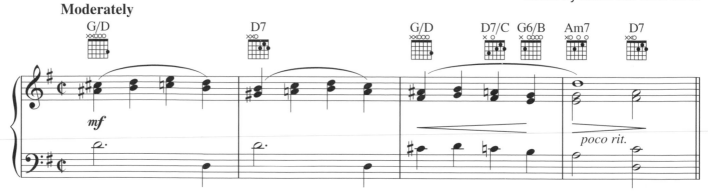

In Ve- ro- na my late cous- in Ro- me- o _____

Was three times as stu- pid as my Dro- mi- o. _____

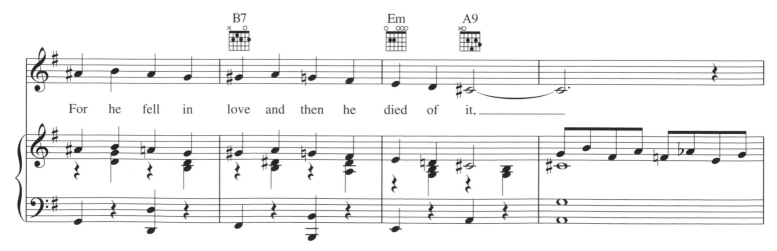

For he fell in love and then he died of it, _____

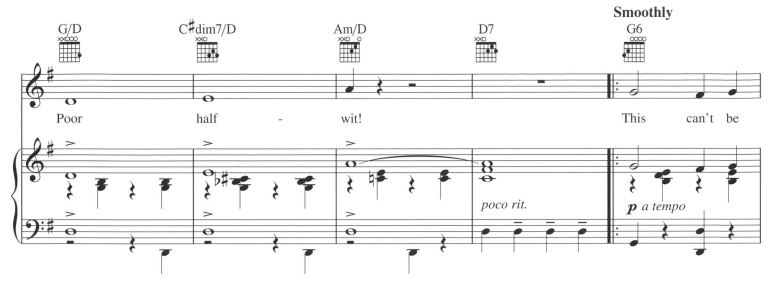

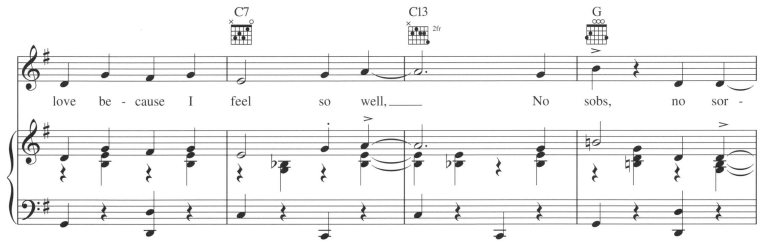

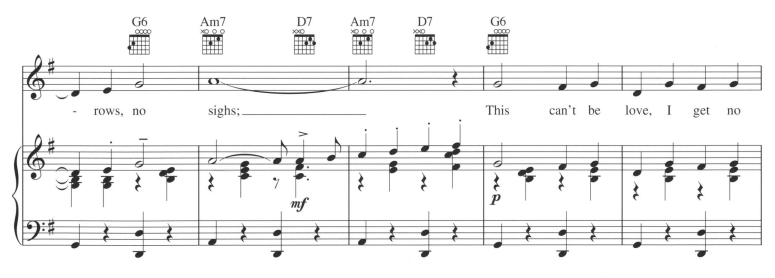

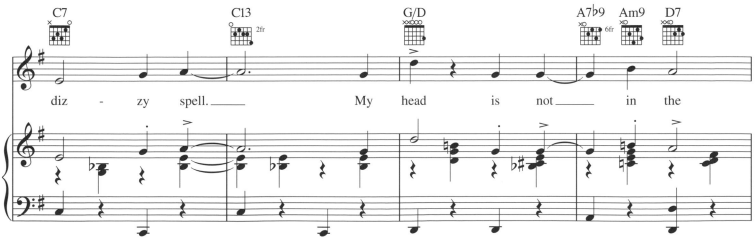

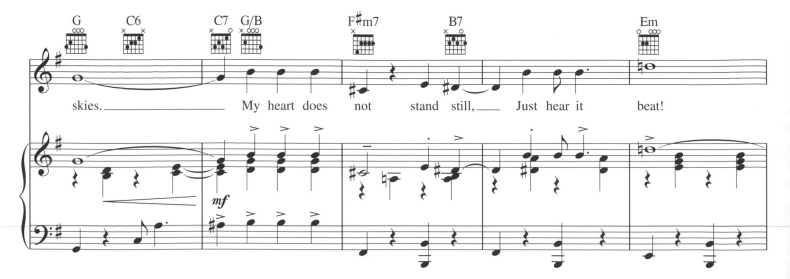

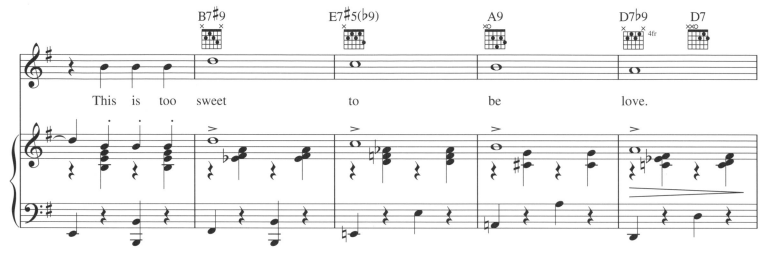

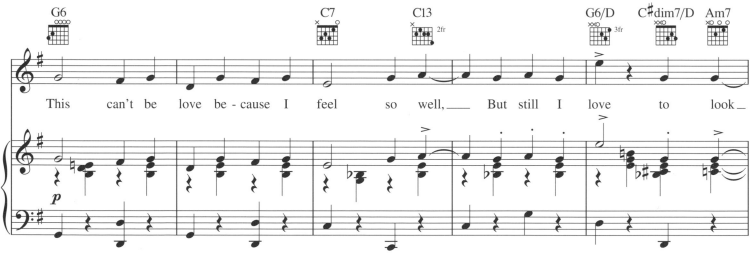

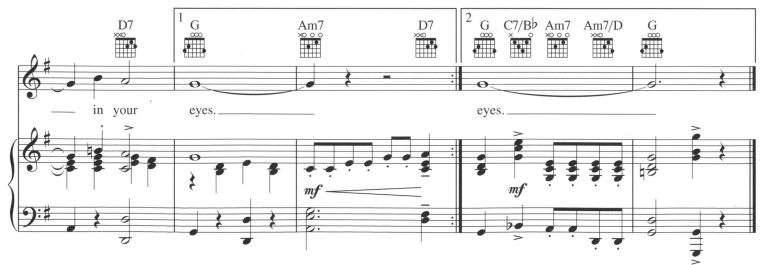